Introduction to
Parish Liturgy

Introduction to

PARISH LITURGY

Rev. Gordon E. Truitt

Celebration Books

Kansas City, Missouri

*To the people
of the Church of Baltimore,
who have permitted me
to preside at their worship,
and who have taught me
how to pray*

Portions of this book were privately printed under the
title, *Parish Liturgy Handbook*, by the Division of
Liturgy of the Archdiocese of Baltimore.

Library of Congress Catalog Card Number: 79-89488

ISBN: 0-934134-02-2

Chapter head illustrations: Miriam Pollard, O.C.S.O.

CONTENTS

Introduction

Over 15 years ago, Vatican II called for "full, conscious, and active participation" in the liturgy by all believers. At first, this call by the bishops gathered in Rome evoked a measure of confusion and a raft of "technical" questions: What do we do first? And what do we do after that?

Now, we have answered many of those technical questions. The liturgical books have been revised, and most Americans have become at least somewhat familiar with the structure of the various rites. With this familiarity, a whole new set of questions has arisen: Why are we doing what we do? What does it mean? Are these rites really conducive to prayer?

Many communities are now struggling with these questions. Most parishes have realized the value of having a planning team. This team is frequently charged with the older, technical questions, phrased now in more immediate terms: What do we do next week? Or, next Advent or Lent?

This book's purpose is twofold. On one level, it provides a summary of the major rites a parish community will experience, suggestions for planning the celebration of those rites, and notes on the liturgical year and popular devotions. On another level, the book tries to lead the reader into a deeper, "spiritual" understanding of the liturgy: the public, communal and ritual expression of the "mystery of faith."

What we are about, as church, is sharing in and expressing the *mysterion*, that indefinable but necessary union of all humanity with and in the Trinity. Liturgy is the point at which we come together to celebrate that union, the time we set aside to see how our whole lives express (or should express!) that mystery, the "sacred space" in which we deepen our union and experience the joy of God's kingdom.

This description may not sound like your parish at Sunday worship, but don't despair yet. That description is an ideal, a challenge, a hope. Occasionally, the signs we use do speak clearly, the veil parts, and we experience mystical union with God. But most of the time, we have to struggle with our own weariness and inattention, with the "density" of the physical signs and the inadequacy of human language, with the overwhelming fact that the church is not yet the fullness of the kingdom. But this is the human and Christian condition. We are, and always will be, a "pilgrim church," *on the way* to the kingdom.

Until the kingdom comes, we work with what we have, however inadequate and fractious the material may be. The church's liturgy is that material. It is a task that we take up, trying to make the physical speak the spiritual, trying to make the everyday speak eternity, trying to make the commonplace reveal the mystery. Liturgy is also our joy, because of the Lord's promise—I will be with you. This *is* my Body, my Blood. Our job, simply, is to be faithful to the promise and the task. Both are what this book is about.

Abbreviations

GIRM	*General Instruction of the Roman Missal*
GICI	*General Instruction on Christian Initiation*
RCIA	*Rite of Christian Initiation of Adults*
GILH	*General Instruction on the Liturgy of the Hours*
MCW	*Music in Catholic Worship*
EAW	*Environment and Art in Catholic Worship*
GIHC	*General Introduction to Holy Communion*

The Local Assembly

In the church's early days, there was no such thing as a "parish." There were only dioceses, presided over by a bishop, assisted by his council (the presbyters, or priests) and the order of deacons (and, occasionally, deaconesses). There were other "orders" in the diocese that helped with various aspects of the church's life: lectors, acolytes, cantors, widows, and men and women dedicated to a life of virginity.

In those times, the whole local church gathered around the bishop on the Lord's Day, to conduct community business, and to celebrate the eucharist. There was only one mass on Sunday. Since Sunday was a working day, mass was celebrated early in the morning, so that everyone (including the bishop!) could get to work on time.

As the church grew, there were too many members to gather in one place at one time. So the bishop's council (the priests) was given responsibility for smaller, local churches—the parishes. In each parish, there was only one Sunday eucharist, presided over by a priest, assisted by his deacons and other local ministers. In time, multiple Sunday masses in each parish became the normal practice, even at the cathedral church. With the increase in masses and the decline in available ministers, the priest became the sole minister of the liturgy, taking on more and more of the roles originally performed by various members of the "orders" in the church.

The liturgical reform of Vatican II has corrected, at least in theory, some of the "parochialism" that crept into the life of parishes over the years. The *General Instruction of the Roman Missal* (GIRM) points out (no. 74), **"Among the various ways of celebrating the eucharist in the local church,** first place should be given to mass at which the bishop presides with the college of presbyters and the ministers, and with the people taking full and active part."

This is the primary, most ancient model of the church at worship. The bishop is the chief liturgist of the diocese, and his is the major liturgy in the diocese. It is the "principle sign of the church" (GIRM, no. 74). Every parish liturgy is modeled on and related to the bishop's liturgy. The Episcopal Church symbolizes this relationship by keeping a special bishop's throne in the sanctuary of every church, as a sign that he presides over the life of even the smallest and most remote parish. While the ideal in each parish would be one Sunday liturgy at which everyone would take part, this is not possible in many parishes. We need at least two to three masses each weekend. This reality reduces the sign value of the assembly even further, since it can happen that even parish members who regularly attend one mass may never see their bishop performing his chief function —presiding over the liturgy and preaching the gospel.

In thinking about the liturgy, we must remember that *this* group, gathered for the 9:15 Sunday mass, is a sign of the whole parish gathered for worship. And each parish, in turn, is a sign of the *whole* local church (the diocese) gathered around its bishop. The clearer these relationships become for those responsible for parish worship, the easier it will be to recognize the parish's relationship to the bishop and, through him, to the universal church.

The functions of the local assembly

In the second chapter of the Acts of the Apostles, Luke described an ideal gathering of the local church. According to Acts 2:42, the assembly on the Lord's Day had a four-fold function: to hear the apostles teach (the Greek word is *didake*), to share the common life (*koinonia*), to break bread (*eucharistia*), and to pray. Over the centuries, many of these tasks were siphoned off to various groups in the parish or the diocese, so that the only thing left in many instances was the "breaking of bread."

Because of the complexity of modern life, it is probably impossible to return to those simple days. However, it is important to remember that *all* the tasks mentioned above—teaching, community life, prayer, plus service (*diakonia*), need to be related to the gathering on Sunday for the eucharist.

If liturgy is to regain its rightful place in the church's life, the whole life of the parish and the diocese must be seen as leading to or following from the church's life of prayer. In the words of Vatican II's *Constitution on the Sacred Liturgy* (no. 10), liturgy *must* be the "summit toward which the activity of the church is directed; at the same time it is the fountain from which all her power flows." Besides being the place at which the church assembles to offer worship, liturgy performs a very pragmatic function—it is the mortar that binds together the scattered life of the local church. No other part of the church's life has this power of unifying and focusing our diverse activities. No other action has the power to proclaim that the "sovereignty of the world has passed to our Lord and to his Christ" (Revelation 11:15).

Ministers to the assembly's worship

In different ways, the ordained and unordained ministers assist the worship of the local assembly of the church. First among these, of course, is the bishop, who stands as a sign of unity within the local church, and between his diocese and the universal church. Within the diocese, the bishop has a special mandate to work so that "all those committed to (his) care may be of one mind in prayer and through the reception of the sacraments may grow in grace and be faithful witnesses to the Lord" (Vatican II, *Decree on the Bishops' Pastoral Office in the Church*, no. 15).

Within the diocese, there is an office or a group to assist the bishop in this pastoral liturgical ministry. Identified variously as the diocesan liturgical commission, office of worship, liturgy office, or division of liturgy, it provides the bishop with the information he needs to be the chief liturgist. This group also works with the parishes and other diocesan organizations, offices, and institutions, to deepen their understanding of the liturgical renewal and their love for every opportunity to gather in worship of the Lord.

There are ordained ministers in the parishes—priests and deacons—charged with presiding over and encouraging community worship. Vatican II's *Decree on the Ministry and Life of Priests* (no. 6) says:

> To the degree of their authority and in the name of their bishop, priests exercise the office of Christ the Head and the Shepherd. Thus they gather God's family together as a brotherhood of living unity, and lead it through Christ and in the Spirit to God the Father. For the exercise of this ministry, as for other priestly duties, spiritual power is conferred upon them for the upbuilding of the church.

Like the bishop in the diocese, the priest in the parish should be a sign and source of unity and spiritual growth. To preside over the sacraments, he needs to understand his role, especially in relationship to the other ministries and to the basic ministry of the congregation itself—to be the Body of Christ.

Deacons have a variety of tasks to perform, summed up as ministry "in the liturgy, of the word, and of charity." (*Dogmatic Constitution on the Church*, no. 29). At the eucharist, the deacon "proclaims the gospel, sometimes preaches God's word, leads the general intercessions of the faithful, assists the priest or bishop, gives communion to the faithful . . . , and sometimes gives directions to the congregation" (GIRM, no. 61). The deacon may also assist with the sacraments of baptism and marriage, funerals and burial services. He is responsible for teaching scripture, presiding occasionally over the Liturgy of the Hours and other forms of prayer, and administering viaticum to the dying. He is also responsible, when possible, for the *diakonia* of the local church—care of the poor, the weak and the defenseless.

There are other important ministries the liturgy calls forth in the parishes. These are necessary, not just to "give the people something to do," but to reveal the nature of our worship as *community worship*—not the sole preserve of any one order within the church. These ministries include:

Lector or reader. This person is the living voice of God in the proclamation of the word.

Acolyte. This minister assists the priest and deacon, and distributes communion. This ministry includes more than the role of the "server" or "altarboy"—more a "master of ceremonies," who makes sure everything is ready and the service flows smoothly.

Cantor and other music ministers. Those who prepare, present, and lead the singing of music perform a definite ministry for the community. Chief among this group is the cantor, who sings the liturgical texts (responsorial psalm, alleluia verse, the *Exsultet*, when necessary, and other texts not proper to the congregation, the priest or the deacon).

Ushers. This group welcomes the members of the congregation and makes them comfortable, providing them with materials for the service, taking up the collection, assisting with the communion procession, the procession with gifts, etc.

Other ministers as needed (godparents, sponsors, dancers, artists, etc.).

One large group of ministers in parish worship is the parish liturgy planning team, or liturgy committee or commission. The *General Instruction* (no. 73) says: "All concerned should work together in preparing the ceremonies, pastoral arrangements, and music for each celebration. They should work under the direction of the rector and should consult the people about the parts which belong to them."

This committee or team has several functions to perform:

Educational. The committee should itself be informed about the nature of the liturgy (especially the eucharist) and should be familiar with the liturgical books. In turn, it should work to inform the members of the congregation about the history and nature of Catholic worship;

Liturgical. This group should assist in the planning of major services and, whenever possible, with the planning of Sunday eucharist (or at least with the "major" Sunday liturgy). The members should also make themselves available to guarantee that the planned service runs smoothly and clearly includes all the members of the assembly;

Spiritual. Within and beyond the liturgy itself, this group should assist as much as possible in deepening the parish prayer life, by encouraging prayer groups, scripture study groups, devotions and other forms of prayer.

Who should be on the planning team? There are obvious members—one or more members of the clergy staff, one or more members of the music team, the head lector and the head usher. Others should be added depending on the parish or the particular services being planned—members of the Altar Guild, or artists, or a liaison with the parish council, members of the congregation, etc. Basically, the team should include persons who will develop good liturgy appropriate for the congregations gathered for worship.

Some parishes separate the liturgy planning team from the parish liturgy committee. If you look over the tasks outlined earlier, you will notice that some of them are long-range projects (education and concern for the parish's spiritual life). These projects could be handled by a liturgy committee which would meet quarterly. The more direct planning projects could be the work of smaller planning teams, each with responsibility for one of the major liturgies (e.g., the "choir mass" and the "folk mass" planning teams). These teams would be responsible to the larger committee, with the task of "oversight"—coordinating all the parish liturgical functions.

This division of labor would clarify the work to be done, and could also cut down on the number of meetings to be held (a definite benefit to all involved!).

The Liturgical Year

Psychologists and psychiatrists teach the importance of the cycles of birth and death in the growth of the human person from childhood to adulthood. Each of us has a "biological clock," a personal rhythm for eating, sleeping, working, and resting. There is a rhythm in the earth itself, in the changes of the seasons and in the movement of continents and glaciers. Life is movement, growth and decline, light and dark, death and renewal.

It is not surprising, then, that there is rhythm and movement in our shared Christian life. It becomes visible in the initiation of new members and in the funeral celebrations of those who have died, in the reconciliation of sinners and in marriages and ordinations. It is visible, too, through the cycles of the liturgical year, cycles manifested in the eucharist where we "proclaim the death of the Lord, until he comes" (1 Corinthians 11:26).

This rhythm is important only if it speaks to us, if we sense it. We must see the various sacraments as revealing the cycles, not just in individual lives, but in the life of the whole community. We must take account of the liturgical year which helps to shift our attention as it highlights various elements in the saving mystery of Christ's presence, his dying and rising to lead us to the Father.

The Easter Triduum

The three day celebration of covenant renewal is the heart of the liturgical year. The mass of the Lord's Supper on Holy Thursday, the celebration of the Lord's Passion on Good Friday, and the Easter Vigil during the night of Holy Saturday-Easter Sunday—these three events are the year's most ancient part. It shows what we are about as Christians—our dying and rising with Christ, our entry into God's kingdom. In the early Middle Ages, a candidate for ordination to the priesthood had to be able to do two things—"read a Mass" and compute the date of Easter. The second skill was essential, because all time was counted from this day—backward to the first Sunday of Advent, and forward to the last Sunday after Pentecost. All other feasts of the year look to this Triduum for their meaning, and every Sunday is a mini-celebration of the covenant renewal.

Lent: season of repentance and renewal

Lent is a 40 day period first instituted as a time for catechumens to make their final preparation for initiation into the community at the Easter Vigil. With the development of the practice of penance in the third and fourth centuries, Lent took on a more penitential note. Penitents were excluded from the community while they did penance. They were reconciled to the community during the Triduum, either on Holy Thursday or Good Friday. With the decline in adult baptisms, and the decrease in public penance in the sixth and seventh centuries, Lent became a time for the whole community to practice penance and to renew its commitment to Christ. *Both* these notes, repentance and renewal, mark our contemporary Lenten practices, reinforced in the readings for the Sunday Lenten liturgies.

Easter season: unfolding the mysteries

As Lent was the time of preparation for intiation, so the 50 days from Easter to Pentecost were a time for "mystagogical catechesis"—for helping the newly-baptized understand what had happened to them, what it meant to be a Christian, and what the rites themselves meant. This period ended, as it ends now, with the celebration of the Holy Spirit's continuing presence in the Body of Christ, the church. Because the Easter Season does not end with Ascension Thursday, the sign of Easter—the paschal candle—should remain in the sanctuary until Pentecost Sunday.

Christmas and the Christmas season

Christmas is more than Jesus' birthday; it is about the mystery of the incarnation. That is why the Christmas feast is followed (after the feast of the Holy Family) by the Epiphany (Christ's revelation to the nations) and the Baptism of the Lord (Jesus' public declaration of his ministry, and the Father's sealing of his Son with the Holy Spirit). Jesus is not simply the Babe of Bethlehem, but "one who, because of his likeness to us, has been tested in every way, only without sin." (Hebrews 4:15)

Advent: preparing for the appearance of Christ

The four weeks of Advent are, of course, a time to prepare to celebrate Christ's birth. But the Advent readings remind us that *each* liturgical year looks forward to a second coming, as does each celebration of the eucharist —"until he comes." The beginning of the liturgical year places us in the "end time" or in "eschatological time"—the time of the kingdom, and of Christ's final victory. Our Advent prayer is always, "Thy kingdom come!"

Ordinary time

The Sundays outside the four great seasons are called "Sundays in Ordinary Time" (in the *Sacramentary*) or "Sundays of the Year" (in the *Lectionary*). They are not extra-ordinary, in the sense they do not highlight in an outstanding way the mysteries of salvation. But they are the weekly celebrations of the Lord's death and resurrection, the highlight of our weekly life in Christ. There are normally 33 or 34 of these Sundays. The last Sunday of Ordinary Time (the Sunday before Advent) looks to Christ's reign over space and time, and is called the Solemnity of Christ the King.

Solemnities in ordinary time

There are certain solemnities of Christ, Mary and the saints that replace the Sunday observance in Ordinary Time. They emphasize mysteries of the

Lord or of Mary not commemorated in the great seasons, or particular saints or events central to the mystery of life in Christ or to the mystery of the church. They are:

January 1: Solemnity of Mary, Mother of God

February 2: Feast of the Presentation of the Lord

Sunday after the Solemnity of the Holy Trinity: Corpus Christi

June 24: Solemnity of the Birth of John the Baptist

June 29: Solemnity of Peter and Paul, Apostles

August 6: Feast of the Transfiguration

August 15: Solemnity of the Assumption

September 14: Feast of the Triumph of the Holy Cross

November 1: Solemnity of All Saints

November 2: All Souls' Day

November 9: Feast of the Dedication of St. John Lateran

December 25: Solemnity of Christmas

The cycles of readings

The Sunday *Lectionary* is arranged in a three year cycle of texts. The purpose is twofold. The Old Testament reading and the gospel harmonize somewhat thematically. The second (or New Testament) reading is usually semi-continuous—it goes through one book or letter, before moving to another book of the New Testament. This arrangement provides two separate sources for themes, music, homily, etc.

Each of the cycles (A, B, and C) has its own "feel." The following information is drawn from the Introduction to the *Lectionary* (nos. 11-16).

Advent. The Advent Sunday gospels are arranged thematically: First Sunday, the Lord's coming in glory at the end of time; Second and Third Sundays, John the Baptist; Fourth Sunday, the events which immediately prepared for the Lord's birth. The Old Testament readings are prophecies about the messiah and messianic times, especially those taken from the book of

Isaiah. The selections from the writings of the apostles present exhortations and instructions on different themes of this season.

Christmas Season. The readings on these Sundays speak of the mystery celebrated on that Sunday.

Lent. The gospel readings are arranged this way: First and Second Sundays, the Lord's temptation and the transfiguration as recorded in the Synoptic gospels; Third to Fifth Sundays: Year A (from the gospel of John)—the Samaritan woman, the man born blind, and the raising of Lazarus (these readings, central to initiation, may replace the readings of the B and C cycles); Year B—John's text about Christ's future glorification through his cross and resurrection; Year C—Luke's texts on conversion.

Easter Season. Until the third Sunday of Easter the gospel selections recount the appearances of the risen Christ. The story of the Good Shepherd appears on the Fourth Sunday. The gospel pericopes of the fifth to seventh Sundays are excerpts from the teaching and prayer of Christ after the Last Supper. The first reading on each Sunday is from the Acts of the Apostles, arranged to show the life, growth, and witness of the early church. The selections from the writings of the apostles are: Year A, First Letter of Peter; Year B, First Letter of John; Year C, the Book of Revelation.

Ordinary Time. Basically, the gospel texts are semi-continuous arrangements of each of the Synoptic gospels: Matthew in Year A, Mark in Year B (with a special insert of John's teaching on the Bread of Life for Sundays 17-21), and Luke in Year C. The Old Testament readings were chosen to harmonize with the gospel readings in each cycle. For the second reading on each Sunday, a semi-continuous reading of the letters of Paul and James is presented. First Corinthians is spread across the three-year cycle because of its length, and the Letter to the Hebrews is divided between Year B and Year C.

The Weekday Cycles. There is a two-year cycle for the first reading in Ordinary Time, chosen from either Testament, depending on the length of the books to be read. The gospel readings are arranged so that Mark is read first (weeks 1-9), then Matthew (weeks 10-21), and finally Luke (weeks 22-34).

Tables. To find the cycle for Sundays and weekdays, consult the tables in the front of the *Lectionary*. For the three-year Sunday cycle, Year C is a year whose number is equally divisible by three (e.g., 1977), as if the cycle began with the first year of the Christian era. For the two-year weekday cycle, odd-numbered years are Year I, even-numbered years are Year II.

Eucharist

In the introduction to his masterwork, *The Mass of the Roman Rite (Missarum Sollemnia)*, Joseph Jungmann writes:

> Even since the God-Man walked this earth of ours and closed His career with the redemptive sacrifice of the Cross, there has been in the midst of men that mystery-filled renewal of His world-saving offering which has continued from age to age and from land to land, and which will so continue till He comes again. Sometimes with pomp and splendor in the midst of thousands, sometimes in the quiet of a lonely chapel, in the poverty of a tiny village church, in some out-of-the-way spot from which men consecrated to God go out to their works of love, everywhere the same mystery is daily consummated in endless repetition . . . . A mighty process of assimilation, tending ever farther and farther, is centered in this glowing hearth—a process of conformation or at least of approximation of the earthly to the heavenly, of the sinful life of man to the offering of the Son of God to His Father's will.

This is our eucharist—a reentry into the mystery of Christ's dying and rising, a sharing in the one perfect sacrifice that effects our liberation from failure, our union with the Father in his Son through the Holy Spirit. It takes its shape from its Jewish origin in a sacred banquet, and it draws its power from the past (the cross and the empty tomb) and the future (the promised wedding feast of the Lamb in God's kingdom). Its language is of the present, its symbols and its gestures come from a long and venerable history. It is made present here, in the gathering of the faithful who "do" or "make" eucharist in this place and in this time. It is the "mystery of faith" which we endlessly proclaim, and to which we are joined as members of the Body of Christ, through our baptism, for the world's salvation.

This event has many titles. It is the "breaking of bread," the "Lord's Supper," the "eucharist, or great thanksgiving," the "Divine Liturgy," the "mass," "communion." Every eucharist is of world-shaking significance, since the proclamation of the gospel depends on the Lord's continued power and presence among his people. The people formed around the Lord's table become the sign of God's overwhelming love for all men and women in every age.

The willingness to share in eucharist, and to receive the Lord's body and blood, has consequences more terrible and awe-inspiring than any other human decision. It is a sign of our unity with Christ's mission, a renewal of the covenant sealed in Jesus' life, death, and resurrection—God's choice to speak with a human voice, to act with human gestures, to let every event of human life speak the mystery, to let the sharing of bread and wine speak the unspeakable, the ineffable, God's own commitment to our salvation and our union with him.

From ancient times, the liturgy of the eucharist has been joined to the liturgy of the word, forming what the *General Instruction of the Roman Missal* (no. 8) calls "one act of worship." The proclamation of the scriptures, especially the gospel, draw us into the meaning of Christ's presence, which we sign and join through the eucharist. The two events—word and eucharist—interact with each other in the community. Full and conscious sharing in the mystery of word and sacrament is the goal for the members of the community of faith.

This is the mystery given into human hands. We must prepare, meditate, celebrate and live it in our dying and rising.

The structure of eucharist

The liturgy of the word and the liturgy of the eucharist are surrounded with minor, transition rites, an introduction, the preparation of the altar and gifts and concluding rites. The present structure looks like this:

Introductory (minor) rites:
> Entrance song (or music or silence)
> Sign of the cross and greeting
>> (may be followed by a brief introductory statement)
> Choice of:
>> Rite of blessing and sprinkling holy water
>> *or:* penitential rite A, B, or C
> Hymn of praise (*Gloria*) (omitted in some seasons)
> Opening prayer

Liturgy of the word
> First (Old Testament) reading
>> (from New Testament in certain seasons)
> Responsorial psalm
>> (sung or recited in different ways)
> Second (New Testament) reading
> Period for silent reflection
> Gospel acclamation (Alleluia)
>> (*must* be sung—when not sung, omit)
> Gospel reading
> Homily
> Profession of faith (creed)
>> (replaced by baptismal promises on Easter)
> General intercessions (prayer of the faithful)

Preparation of altar and gifts (minor rites)
> Procession with gifts (may be accompanied by music)
> Vesting of the altar
> Preparation of the gifts
>> (in silence, or with music)
> Prayer over the gifts

Liturgy of the eucharist

The eucharistic prayer
Preface
The prayer
(choice of nine; the acclamations should be sung)

The communion rites
Lord's prayer and embolism ("Deliver us, Lord")
Sign of peace
Communion procession
Time for quiet meditation
Prayer after communion

Concluding (minor) rites
Blessing
Dismissal
(There may be a final hymn or other music)

The entrance rites

As the outline shows, we have six separate entrance rites. This part of the service should be as brief and clear as possible. It is only the beginning, a transition from our concerns into the liturgy (something we should take sufficient time to do by coming early to church for personal prayer and reflection).

The proclamation of scripture

The liturgy of the word is *not* a course in scripture studies. It is a *celebration* of God's word, present among his people. As the *General Instruction of the Roman Missal* puts it (no. 9), "When the scriptures are read in the church, God himself speaks to his people, and it is Christ, present in his word, who proclaims the gospel." The lector and the deacon or priest are to be the living voice of God speaking to his people. We must take seriously God's chosen way of communication with us—through a living human voice. It is the incarnational principle in action. Reading the scriptures in private, without hearing them spoken in the midst of the community, is a second class way of receiving the word.

The homily

The homily is, in a sense, the spoken assent of the community to the proclaimed word. It is not so much an exegesis of scripture as an attempt to "hear what the Spirit is saying to the churches" (Revelation 2:29f). It is a kind of spoken meditation on what God is saying to *this* community, a sharing of prayerful insight into the word's meaning. While it is normally the celebrant's role to give the homily (GIRM, no. 42), he should be willing to pray over the readings and share reflections with other community members, in preparation for his role as spokesperson for the community's meditation.

The general intercessions

The general intercessions conclude the liturgy of the word. They are "general" because this prayer intercedes for the whole church and for the needs of all men and women (cf. GIRM, no. 45). They may include specific mention of individuals or groups in the congregation, but these should be included as part of a general prayer (e.g., "for the sick, especially N."). This prayer should never be a kind of "shopping list" of local needs. Usually, the prayer should include petitions for the needs of the church, for public authorities and the salvation of the world, for those oppressed by any need, and then for the local community (cf. GIRM, no. 46).

The preparation of the altar and the gifts

There are two major signs in this minor transition rite between the liturgy of the word and the liturgy of the eucharist. The first is the procession of the people with the gifts; the second is the preparation of the altar and the placing of the gifts on it. The prayers that accompany the placing of the gifts are *not* prayers of offering (the offering is done during the eucharistic prayer), and so they need not be said aloud. The gesture of placing the gifts is *not* a gesture of offering, and so the gifts should not be held high above the altar.

A word about gifts: where possible, the gifts really should come from the people. Occasionally, certainly for special occasions, a family can bake a loaf of unleavened bread, or provide the wine to be used for eucharist.

The eucharistic prayer

"The eucharistic prayer, a prayer of thanksgiving and sanctification, is the center and high point of the entire celebration" (GIRM, no. 54). The prayer begins with the introductory dialogue of the preface, and concludes with the doxology and the great Amen. In all the eucharistic prayers, except those for masses with children, there are three acclamations for the people, by which they give their assent to the prayer's words and actions, and sign their willingness to be joined to Christ's offering. These three are: the seraphic hymn (Holy, holy, holy), the anamnesis or memorial acclamation, and the great Amen. They should normally be sung.

The outline of a model eucharistic prayer is as follows (cf. GIRM, no. 55):

Thanksgiving—contained especially in the preface, it gives a "motive" for this celebration of the eucharist, by mentioning some particular aspect of salvation, or the whole work of salvation. The preface is followed by the first acclamation.

Epiclesis—the invocation of the Holy Spirit over the gifts, since it is by the Sprit's work the bread and wine become Christ's body and blood and the eucharist becomes effective for our salvation.

Words of institution (consecration)—the words of institution are drawn from all four accounts of the Last Supper in the New Testament, and they are followed by Christ's command which instituted the eucharist: to "do the memory" of him. The words of institution are followed by the second acclamation (the anamnesis or memorial acclamation).

Anamnesis-offering—we recall the reason for the Lord's Supper by specific reference to the passion, death, and resurrection, and point to the completion of this meal in the kingdom through reference to the ascension and the Lord's return in glory. Once the full context of the sacrifice has been identified, we then offer this gift of the Lord to the Father, and join ourselves to the offering of this perfect sacrifice.

Second Epiclesis—in some of the eucharistic prayers, there is a second invocation of the Holy Spirit over the people assembled for this eucharist, since, again, it is the Spirit who makes us one with Christ's sacrifice.

Intercessions—these brief intercessions lay out the offering's purpose: united to the whole church, on earth and in heaven, living and dead, we pray for the salvation of the whole world.

Final Doxology—the trinitarian doxology, and the gesture of offering which accompanies it, summarize the prayer: through, with, and in Christ, in the power of the Holy Spirit, we offer all honor and glory to the Father. The final doxology (the Great Amen) gives the people's assent to the prayer, and is a sign of their willingness to be united to Jesus' offering.

Each of the nine eucharistic prayers has its own "flavor," which, to some extent, determines their use at a specific service. Four prayers are found in the *Sacramentary*. The other five are for "interim" use only, and may be dropped or replaced at the end of the three year period of experimentation. Two prayers are for masses with the theme of reconciliation, and the other three are for masses with children. Here is a brief summary of these nine prayers:

Eucharistic prayer I (the Roman Canon), the second oldest of our present prayers, is strong on intercession and the notion of sacrifice; it is the least clear in its outline.

Eucharistic prayer II, the prayer with the oldest "model," is based on the Prayer of Hippolytus from *The Apostolic Tradition* (early third century). It is also the shortest, and has the clearest outline. It emphasizes the offering of bread and wine, and our sharing in Christ's body and blood.

Eucharistic prayer III emphasizes Christ's offering through all ages, in all lands, into eternity. It stresses our unity with Christ's sacrifice.

Eucharistic prayer IV, the only one with an invariable preface, is the most "scriptural" of the prayers, providing a summary of Christ's saving work and relating his sacrifice to his ministry.

Reconciliation prayer I places the notion of reconciliation in a cosmic context, and uses the image of the cross as the sign of reconciliation.

Reconciliation prayer II points out the present needs for reconciliation, the "tasks" to which this eucharist should lead us.

Prayer for children I uses the seraphic hymn (Holy, holy, holy) frequently through a very long preface that summarizes God's work on our behalf—creation, Jesus' ministry, the church.

Prayer for children II uses frequent acclamations throughout, and leaves a place for specific petitions. It centers on Jesus' ministry.

Prayer for children III provides for frequent acclamations, either the one in the text "or some other suitable acclamation of praise." It offers inserts for various seasons and occasions (Easter ones are provided), and emphasizes church unity.

The communion rites

This rite's various elements express our unity with each other and with Christ. We are united by praying the prayer Jesus taught us. United in prayer, we make the sign of unity in the Body of Christ, the church—the sign of peace. And then we join in the sign of our total unity with Christ, communion in his body and blood.

As often as possible, communion should be distributed under both forms as a fuller sign of our communion with Christ. Communion from the cup is preferred over intinction.

Planning for Sunday eucharist

Obviously, not everything can be done for every Sunday celebration. Some parishes will be able to spend more time in planning than others, because they have more resources for developing their liturgies. Here are some basic principles to be observed whenever a group sits down to plan liturgy:

Do what you can. Don't give up because your parish has not reached the ideal. Only Jesus and the saints have accomplished this goal.

Push for more than you can. None of us is really fully aware of his/her limits. We can always do more than we think, and be better than we believe. After all, the Spirit has promised to work through us.

Plan carefully. Make sure you have covered as many points as you can, and try to think of everything. You won't, but that gives you something to work on next time. Also, try to plan well in advance. This will give you more time to be satisfied with what you have done, and think of contingencies you haven't yet considered.

Work with the community you have. Each parish has its "personality," its development in the life of faith. In fact, each Sunday congregation has a different "feel." The congregation at the early mass is different from the folk mass gathering, is different from the choir mass, is different from the Saturday evening crowd, etc. These differences can be an asset to planning, if the team works carefully on the sense of faith these various congregations express in their worship.

Here are some places to start your planning for a particular congregation or special service or season.

Begin with the assigned readings. This is a good place to discover a unifying theme, especially during the great seasons. A theme is not absolutely necessary, but it can help to unify a service. (Sometimes, the responsorial psalm will reveal a common theme in the readings.) Based on the theme, decide which eucharistic prayer and which preface are appropriate for this celebration.

Decide how the readings will be done. Is there any special way to highlight the important verses? Should you have a procession with the gospel book? Decide on the other options for the liturgy of the word: especially in the introductory rites.

Decide which acclamations should be sung. What text and music should be used? The following should normally be sung: the responsorial psalm, the gospel acclamation (alleluia), the seraphic hymn (Holy, holy, holy), the memorial acclamation, the great Amen. Other prayers and acclamations should be sung occasionally: the *Gloria*, the Lord's prayer, the Lamb of God.

Decide on other elements which will add to the prayerful celebration of the eucharist—the form of the final blessing, other music, hymns, acclamations, the setting for the eucharist (banners, lighting, etc.).

Write down what you have decided. Make sure that everyone involved in ministering knows what is expected of him/her. Keep a copy for later reference.

Planning is particularly important for the Easter Triduum and the great seasons (Advent and Christmas, Lent and Easter). Plan each of these seasons as a unit, so that the preparatory seasons (Advent and Lent) build up to the central feasts of the year (Christmas and the Easter Triduum), and the celebrative seasons (Christmas and Easter) unfold the meaning of the feasts.

Weekday eucharist

While most communities do not have the facilities to plan fully each of the weekday celebrations (nor should they, otherwise we'd wind up with seven Sundays each week), some simple planning can be given to these days, especially to feast of saints important to a congregation. For instance, vary the way in which the responsorial psalm is prayed antiphonally, or alternating verses from one side of the congregation to the other, or having everyone pray the whole psalm, etc. At times, weekday congregations can sing the acclamations, or a hymn after communion. A limited amount of variety in the forms of weekday celebrations can add to the devotion and attention of the worshipping congregation.

Masses (and other celebrations) with children

Most parishes plan masses with children at some time or other. More frequently, they plan paraliturgies (prayer services, penance services, scripture services). In 1973, the Congregation for Divine Worship published the *Directory for Masses with Children* (found in the front of the *Sacramentary*). The *Directory* makes several important points, and offers significant options for planning masses and other celebrations. In concert with the eucharistic prayers for masses with children, it is a rich resource for special liturgies. Some key points made in the *Directory*:

Unity. Children's liturgies should be part of a unified parish program of worship. These special liturgies serve to lead children into more mature forms of worship in the adult congregation.

Frequency. These liturgies should not be too frequent, otherwise they will encourage either boredom or the sense that liturgy must consist of endless variety.

Congregation. In addition to children, there should be some adults present to worship and sometimes to supply the ministries children are not prepared to assume.

Involvement. By word, gesture, music, and silence, the children should be involved in the liturgy's various parts. Movement and gesture especially create this sense of involvement. Everything should not be done *to or for* the children. They should be involved as much as possible in the preparation and celebration of God's saving act on their behalf.

Initiation

Initiation, like *initial* and *initiative,* has a sense of "what comes first," a first step, a beginning. The dictionary defines the verb *initiate* as "to begin, set going, or originate," "to introduce into the knowledge of some art or subject," or "to admit with formal rites into secret knowledge, a society, etc." These meanings relate to the process of Christian initiation. Initiation refers to "what comes first"—the first step into the Christian community, the beginning of Christian life. In the past, we thought of baptism as *the* sacrament of Christian initiation. It was indeed the first step. But, as the dictionary points out, initiation also involves introducing someone into knowledge. There is a catechetical aspect to Christian initiation, tied to the "formal rites" by which a person becomes a member of the church.

The church defines itself by the way it initiates new members into the community of faith. In former times, everyone was baptized shortly after birth. Little weight was put on the rite itself (it was performed almost casually) or on the catechetical program that should have accompanied the rite. In Christendom, it was presumed that people would pick up the faith, almost by osmosis, from the surrounding atmosphere.

But now we are in a new world no longer imbued with Christianity's symbols and language. Christendom as a prevailing culture is long gone. Once more, the process of becoming a Christian, and the rites that symbolize and seal the becoming, take on key importance for the church's life.

The initiation rites define the way we present ourselves to the world. We can no longer take casually the process of becoming Christian. It is a serious and important step, not just for a particular individual, but for the church. What we are symbolizing in the sacraments of initiation is the heart of the mystery of faith. As the *General Introduction to Christian Initiation* (GICI) puts it (nos. 1 and 2):

> Through the sacraments of Christian initiation (baptism, confirmation, and the eucharist) men and women are freed from the power of darkness. With Christ they die, are buried and rise again. They receive the spirit of adoption which makes them God's sons and daughters and, with the entire people of God, they celebrate the memorial of the Lord's death and resurrection. Thus the three sacraments of Christian initiation closely combine to bring the faithful to the full stature of Christ and enable them to carry out the mission of the entire people of God in the Church and in the world.

The three sacraments of baptism, confirmation and eucharist define what the church is about in this world. They are the heart of our worship-life, the center from which our need to catechize grows. In recent years, we have realized the importance of catechizing individuals, families, and the whole community *before* these sacraments are celebrated. We now invite the whole community to the celebration of these sacraments. We are realizing the importance of continuing catechesis *after* the sacraments are celebrated—to unfold the meaning of the events, to make the sacraments themselves the signs that catechesis interprets. Gradually, in many parishes, the notion of initiation, and the sacraments of initiation, are serving to unify the parish life—not just its worship, but also its teaching function, its ministry to the poor and the sick, and its attempts at evangelization and ecumenism.

Adult initiation is the model

For centuries, the church has stated that adult initiation is the model for all other forms of initiation (infant baptism, eucharist, and confirmation for children or adolescents, etc.). But in the ages when not many adults were being initiated, this statement didn't have much impact. Now, however, in our post-Christendom world, it takes on renewed meaning. Our world is not Christian. More and more adults with little or no previous religious training choose to become members of the church. This is especially true in missionary territories, but it is happening as well in "Christian" countries like the United States, where 80 million people have no religious affiliation.

The church has issued a new *Rite of Christian Initiation of Adults* (CIA). It lays out the basic premises about becoming a Christian: it is an event of faith, based on the proclamation of the gospel and the Holy Spirit's work (CIA, no. 1). It is conversion, not just to a set of beliefs, but to the mystery of Christ's dying and rising. As such, it requires prayer, meditation, reflection and intellectual formation (CIA, no. 18-2, and passim). It is a process in which the whole community takes part, because conversion occurs in the "midst of the community of the faithful" (CIA, nos. 4, 41).

From this "spiritual" way of looking at initiation, implications follow for the way the church presents itself and deals with *anyone* wishing full communion. For instance, the parish community must be strong in its faith if it is going to invite new members and catechize them. Likewise, the community worship must be strong and its signs clear, if sacramental life is going to provide the primary symbols from which catechesis develops. Also, other forms of ministry, especially to the poor, the sick and the weak, must be a strong part of parish life, since involvement in these ministries is an essential part of becoming a Christian (CIA, no. 18-2).

Besides this plan for reforming community life, the *Rite of Christian Initiation of Adults* provides a model for catechesis for "inquiring" adults and for all the parish catechetical programs, especially those that revolve around the sacraments. The model includes these points. Any catechesis must involve formation as well as information; prayer, meditation, and service are essential parts of catechesis. Catechesis must involve as much of the community as possible; it is not something which can safely or fruitfully be left only to the "experts," although experts do have an essential role to play. Catechesis is important before the rite, to explain the meaning of what is about to happen; it is equally important *after* the rite has been celebrated, to unfold the implications for Christian living contained in the rite. The rites must be as clear and moving as possible, because they are the "hinges" on which catechesis and Christian living turn; none of the rites of initiation can or should be celebrated "quietly" or "privately"—they should be done with great rejoicing in the midst of the community.

The rite lays out a model for catechesis: pre-catechumenate (or intitial hearing of and response to the word; first evangelization), catechumenate (deep probing into the meaning of faith and the sacraments; careful and well-developed evangelization; the time of "conversion"), purification and enlightenment (or "illumination"—immediate preparation for the sacraments, a kind of "retreat"), celebration of the sacrament(s) (for adult initiation, normally at the Easter Vigil), post-sacramental catechesis or "mystagogia" (explaining the implications of the sacraments for the rest of a person's life in the church).

Baptism of children

If the above holds true, then how do we baptize infants? They cannot be catechized before the sacrament; they undergo no process of conversion. Is the sacrament's meaning nothing more than "washing away original sin" or "saving them from limbo"? No. The celebration of this sacrament depends on several points mentioned above: the faith life of the community; the importance of the sacraments, not just for individuals, but for the life of the community; and the value of post-sacramental catechesis.

Children are, of course, "deserving" of nothing in this world—they have not "earned their right" to anything. Even life is a gift. Certainly the benefits of culture, family love, education, incorporation into the community of parents or peers is also "gift." These gifts are made on the recognition they are important for human life. A child raised by animals (as in the Kipling stories) can never become a mature human being, only an overgrown animal. Children become members of various communities and receive varieties of experiences and education on the basis of their present well-being and their future development (the possibility they will someday improve on these gifts and hand them on in their turn).

The same reasoning explains infant baptism. The greatest gift we can offer is the sharing of our faith through the community's life and worship. No one deserves the gift of faith—it was offered to us "even when we were sinners." We give the experience of life in the community of believers to our children, even though they cannot understand its meaning, *precisely* because it is important to us. It has eminently more value than learning a language, appreciating fine art or learning a skill. From their earliest days, children should be offered this gift, in the hope they will grow to appreciate it, and by their own efforts, advance the church's life in their turn.

This emphasis on the positive values of infant baptism mirrors what we said negatively in the past, when we talked about original sin (a life deprived of its deepest meaning, union with God) and limbo (a lost and unfocused existence, lonely and without value).

The emphasis on the entry into community life and on eventual growth in understanding and celebrating the faith as mature Christian adults has important implications for the way that the baptism of children is celebrated. It is an event important to the *whole* community, and whenever possible it should be celebrated before at least some representatives of the worshipping community (in addition to the family and friends).

It is an event aimed at the child's inclusion in the eucharistic community, and so, at least occasionally, baptism should be celebrated in the context of eucharist. It is an incorporation into the mystery of Christ, and so the best time for celebrating baptism is either during the Easter season or on Sunday. Because it is an important event, it should be carefully planned and celebrated.

Because of baptism's "initiatory" nature, the people who need careful catechesis *before* the sacrament are the parents and the sponsors, since they will be responsible for catechizing the child after the sacrament. The community needs occasional catechesis about the meaning of infant baptism (and other initiation rites), and should be invited to participate in baptisms from time to time. The baptized child needs catechesis appropriate to the stage of development. At first, this will depend on the parents and sponsors, who need support and information from the parish religious educators. Later, it can be handled through the parish religious education programs (for *both* the parents and the children).

Confirmation: the seal of the Spirit

We cannot narrate here the whole history of the meaning and practice of confirmation in the church. The important point is that confirmation is one of the sacraments of initiation, and thus has a close relationship to baptism and eucharist. Through most of the church's history (in fact, until early in the 20th century!) the ancient order of these sacraments was preserved: baptism, confirmation and the eucharist. This order clearly symbolized the gradual movement of people into the eucharistic community, and provided time for catechesis before and after each of these sacraments.

With our present order (baptism, eucharist, confirmation) the relationship is somewhat "deranged." Still, they must all be seen as rites of initiation, and confirmation is now the "sealing" of that process, the sacrament which provides a person with the "power of the Holy Spirit." That power is exercised as the individual matures, in ministry at worship, as a member of the priestly people, in service, and in teaching and proclaiming the gospel.

Like the other sacraments of initiation, confirmation demands a catechesis before the celebration, as well as a post-sacramental catechesis to help the person understand the nature of Christian life and the Spirit's work. The catechesis should reflect confirmation's initiatory nature and its relationship to baptism and eucharist. The catechesis should never suggest confirmation replaces baptism as the sacrament by which one chooses or is chosen for membership in the community.

To highlight confirmation's meaning during the celebration, baptismal signs (renewal of baptismal promises, blessing and sprinkling of holy water, white garment) can be used. Communion should always be under both forms. The chrism should always be well-perfumed, so that its power as a sign of anointing can stand out. The bishop should not hesitate to use the chrism freely. The community should be invited to participate (or, at the very least, to pray for the candidates before confirmation).

Some "firsts"

Some sacraments, of course, are received only once in a lifetime: baptism, confirmation, orders, and, normally, marriage. Other sacraments, because of their centrality in the Christian life, or because of their "healing" nature, are repeated: eucharist, penance, and the anointing of the sick. Because anointing of the sick only deals with cases of serious illness (see p. 38), it will not be familiar to many people, and some Christians may never share in it. But the eucharist and penance are common experiences for all believers. No matter how often these sacraments are received, there is still a "first time" when people are invited to the Lord's table, or when they need to make the signs of forgiveness and reconciliation. These "firsts" need careful attention by a parish worship team, if they are to lead people into a deeper knowledge and love of the mysteries they make present.

First eucharist

The church has always demanded two things of those who present themselves for communion: knowledge of the mysteries of faith, and devotion. This was made clear at the Council of Trent (21st Session, July 16, 1562), in the Code of Canon Law (Canon no. 854), and in contemporary documents (GIRM, nos. 3 and 5). This is why children and their parents should be given careful preparation for first communion. While it is a joyous event the community shares with these young members of Christ's Body, it is also a serious obligation they take upon themselves: to be conformed more and more to the Lord they receive.

The signs used for first communion should reflect this understanding of the moment's seriousness and joy. It is more than a party. While the ritual and the prayers should be geared to the understanding of the children who participate, these children should also sense the reverence and devotion with which the parents, the priest, and the other adults participate in the eucharist.

There are ways of involving the children without collapsing the Lord's supper into Johnny's or Jane's birthday party. The children can be involved in the choice of scripture texts, and can study those texts beforehand. They might even be invited to help bake the bread to be used, and sample the wine beforehand, so they know what it will taste like. They should be involved in decorating the space, whether it be the church building, a small chapel, or their home. Someone (priest, deacon, catechist, parent) might go through the eucharistic prayer to be used, so the child knows what it says and has a sense of its flow. Other appropriate ideas are in the *Directory for Masses with Children.*

First penance

The service of first penance should always be geared to the child. It should be constructed on the principles found in the *Rite of Penance* and in the *Directory for Masses with Children.*

The priest(s) who preside should be known by the children from prior meetings, so that the children will feel welcomed by a familiar person, not a stranger. The readings should be chosen for their appropriateness for children, not for their abstract truth about reconciliation. A story about how Jesus practiced reconciliation, for instance, is better than long theological reflections from John's gospel.

The signs should be clear and involving: prayer gestures, the arrangement of the places for individual reconciliation, the gesture of imposing hands, etc. The service should not be overly long (not over three-quarters of an hour), and this may necessitate three or four first penance services, instead of one big one. The service should invite the children to return, on their own or with a group, to other penitential times and services provided by the parish. The children should not get the impression that they have to come only with their class, or only with their parents.

The best time for first penance is during Lent, when the season's penitential nature can reinforce the sacrament's meaning.

The Other Sacraments

An ancient myth in Judaism says the world's continued existence depends on 30 people, the "just" of every generation. These 30 do not know who they are, or how important they are: they simply *are* totally just. But if there were only 29 in any generation, the Lord would sweep the earth clean, just as he destroyed the cities of the plain when he could not find ten just people in Sodom (Genesis 18:20-33).

The first Christians saw their lives and their worship in a similar way. They did not baptize people into the community and share the Lord's supper simply for their own salvation, or even for the salvation of their brothers and sisters in the church. They did these things for the world's salvation, so there would be people to proclaim the gospel and the presence of the Lord's saving act would continue across time and space. Since those early days, the sacraments have always been rooted in this missionary, salvific goal.

In our time, we may have put too much emphasis on the benefit to the individual in the sacraments (or perhaps the punishment absence from the assembly entails: "You'll go to hell if you miss Sunday mass!"), and not enough emphasis on the fact that we act not merely for ourselves but for the whole world. In the celebration of each sacrament, there is a four-fold orientation. The first, of course, is worship of the Lord in sacramental signs. The second is the salvation of the world and of the local community: "those here present and all your people, and all who seek you with a sincere heart" (eucharistic prayer IV). Finally, there is a focus on the individuals in the community and especially, in some of the sacraments, on the individual or individuals who are the central figures in the rite as at confirmation, marriage or the anointing of the sick.

Since some sacraments are celebrated by what could be considered an "elite" group (friends of the couple at a marriage or family and friends at a first eucharist in the home), we must remember this wider focus. All the sacraments are important for the local church and for the world. Each celebration should have, in some form, this sense of mission and proclamation. No individual or group has the right to say "This is *my* marriage" or "*my* ordination," and make it a closed event. Because of this wider responsibility to and for the church, the local parish or diocese has a right and a duty to guarantee the *proper* celebration of all the rites. Many dioceses and parishes have issued guidelines for the rites, especially baptism, confirmation, marriage, and orders, to ensure, at least minimally, their relationship to the church's universal mission and to parish life and/or diocesan worship.

There are two sacraments and some related rites that set people apart from the community for special ministries in and to the covenant with the Lord. The sacraments are marriage and orders. The rites are those for institution to other ministries (reader and acolyte), and commitment to the "vowed life" of poverty, celibacy, and obedience.

Christian marriage

The sacrament of marriage is, in a sense, the celebration of the "covenant within the covenant." In Ephesians 5:22-33, Paul uses the relationship of Christ to the church to describe the meaning of marriage. He then applies the meaning of marriage to Christ and the church. Marriage is a commitment to share life, even to and through death. This was Jesus' commitment to us. Marriage, then, becomes a sign and sacrament, not just for the couple or the immediate family, but for the whole church—a reminder of the covenant love we share with each other "in Christ Jesus."

Ordination to diaconate and priesthood

Marriage is ministry to the covenant by signing and living the marriage covenant. The sacrament of holy orders is direct ministry to the covenant. The primary function of the ordained ministers is to help the people find and express that most basic ministry: the assembly's four-fold ministry (Acts 2:42; see also above, pp. 4-5).

The vowed life

Within the local parish, there will occasionally be people (nuns and brothers) who have committed themselves to life in a community under the three vows: poverty, celibacy, and obedience. They do this to follow the Lord more closely, "aim at truly evangelical perfection and increase the holiness and apostolic zeal of (the) church" (opening prayer of the ritual mass for religious profession). Because these people are involved in the church's ministry in special ways (teaching, caring for the poor, nursing, etc.), they support the work of the whole church.

Occasionally, because of their close ties with a parish community, they choose to make their religious profession in the parish church, and invite the community to celebrate the dedication of all people who, like Christ, seek to be pure of heart, obedient to God's will, and detached from things for the gospel's sake (cf. the preface for religious profession).

The other ministries

Other liturgical ministries have special rites occasionally celebrated in the parish. The institution of readers and acolytes is reserved to those who have finished a careful preparation for these ministries. At the moment, fully-prepared people are few in number, but there are many who, with a minimum of preparation, fulfill these two ministries. While they cannot be fully "instituted," it is worthwhile to recognize with ceremony those who give time and effort to the community's worship. Official recognition is important not only for readers and acolytes, of course, but also for other ministers: cantors, musicians, choir members, ushers, planners, ministers of the eucharist (who *may* be officially installed in their ministry in a very simple ceremony), teachers and other volunteers.

Some parishes plan a "ministries day" on a particular Sunday. When the readings and the season are appropriate, they gather as many ministers as possible at one or more of the parish masses, and have them recommit themselves to service (much as priests and deacons do at the chrism mass during Holy Week). This renewal of service is followed by fellowship and refreshment for these people who work to improve parish worship.

Reconciliation and healing

Two sacraments reveal the Lord's mercy in a special way because they are directed at the congregation's suffering members: the sacrament of reconciliation (penance) and the anointing of the sick. These sacraments are important, not just for those to whom they are directed, but also for the whole community. When the community recognizes its responsibility to the suffering, the mystery of the Lord's dying and rising takes on its real dimension in parish worship.

The sacrament of penance

Each parish should have a full program of penitential practice, with all three forms of the new rite of penance (reconciliation of individual penitents, reconciliation of several penitents with individual confession and absolution, and reconciliation of several penitents with general confession and absolution), as well as occasional non-sacramental penitential services and the penitential elements of Lent. Such a program demands careful planning, so that the congregation's sinful members come to recognize the nature of their sin, the way it has hurt themselves and others, and the fact that "penance always entails reconciliation with our brothers and sisters who are always harmed by our sins" (Introduction to the rite of penance, no. 5).

Each parish should make available appropriate space for the celebration of this sacrament, especially for the reconciliation of individual penitents in a reconciliation room, with the option of confessing anonymously or facing the priest in dialogue.

In any service, the basic principle in the introduction to the rite of penance must be observed: whatever form of the rite is used, it must be celebrated *properly* (cf. nos. 10, 11, and 31). There must be sufficient time and an appropriate atmosphere for prayer and the hearing of God's word, for minimal direction in Christian living and the choice of an appropriate penance. This rite cannot be hurried, since it deals with the secret places where a person is in pain because of sin. Healing requires wisdom, prudence, a "deep knowledge of God's action in the hearts" of his people, and a spirit of deep and abiding charity (cf. Introduction to the rite of penance, no. 10). The whole spirit of the rite must reflect that attitude and desire for reconciliation.

The anointing of the sick

Like other sacraments, the anointing of the sick achieves its full meaning only within a context, in this instance, the parish's care for the sick through visitation, prayers, work in hospitals and nursing homes, lunch programs, etc. Only in this sense does the sacrament's meaning as the community's prayer for its suffering members take on visibility (Introduction to anointing, nos. 32-37).

The sick have a ministry to perform for the community as well. They are a reminder of the community's need to care; they show by their patience in suffering the meaning of Christ's suffering; by their healing and restoration to the community they are reminders of God's love for us (cf. Introduction to anointing, nos. 1-4).

Parishes should have a communal anointing of the sick occasionally—once or twice a year. This makes the sick more visible to the parish and invites the prayers of the parish for them.

The sacrament is for those who are *seriously* sick, or facing major surgery, or old and beginning to fail. Therefore, as part of the planning, some attempt should be made to identify those people who are truly sick before the service begins (Introduction to the rite, no. 8). Those who are sick, but who do not fall into the category of being "seriously" sick, should *not* be anointed. However, at the service, they can be prayed over with the laying-on of hands.

Those to be anointed should be visited and prayed with well before the service. The anointing of the sick should also be explained to them and to their families at this time, so they clearly understand the sacrament's meaning (Introduction to the rite, nos. 36 and 37). Whether the anointing is to be done communally or individually, members of the congregation should be invited to share in the prayer at this time, so that the sick may know the community cares (Introduction to the rite, no. 34).

The Christian funeral

The *Rite of Funerals* is like the *Rite of Christian Initiation of Adults*—it occurs in stages, at different times and different places. In the funeral rite, there are three distinct but related "moments" or "stations": the vigil for the deceased (or the "Christian wake"), the funeral mass with the final commendation and farewell, and the service at the grave. Each is important, and deals with a certain aspect of the Christian meaning of death and the natural process of mourning.

Some people have found meaning in the vigil or wake as a time for leave-taking, for remembering the good a person has done in life. This is a time for tears and for prayers for the deceased *and* the mourners.

The funeral mass is filled with resurrection joy. The baptismal white pall, the white vestments, the Easter candle and the singing of alleluias, all remind us that death is the entry into life. The pain of separation is very real at this time, and rejoicing should not be overdone to the point of sham. But it is a time when the priest and other ministers can share their faith in the resurrection with the dead person's family.

The service at the grave or tomb is a sign of the church's continuing care for believers even to the moment of burial. Even in death, the body of a Christian deserves special attention because it has been a "vessel of election" and the "temple of the Holy Spirit."

The introduction to the *Rite of Funerals* notes that "if an individual prayer or other text is clearly not appropriate to the circumstances of the deceased person, it is the responsibility of the priest to make the necessary adaptation" (no. 24).

Christians may choose to have their bodies cremated (or donated to science after death). In these cases, the funeral rites are still celebrated, but those texts which refer to the body's presence are eliminated.

The funeral rite ends with the burial. But the care of the mourners should continue. This is the responsibility not only of the priest, but also of other members of the congregation (Introduction to the rite, no. 16).

On certain days, the funeral mass cannot be celebrated. However, even on these days, the other rites of the funeral liturgy may take place. The eucharist should be celebrated for the deceased at the earliest opportunity. These days are: the Easter Triduum (Holy Thursday, on which only the mass of the Lord's supper is permitted in parishes, Good Friday and Holy Saturday, when no mass is permitted except the mass of the Easter vigil), solemnities, and the Sundays of the Advent, Lent and Easter seasons (Introduction to the rite, no. 6).

The Liturgy of the Hours

A tradition handed down from ancient Jewish prayer calls for three pauses in the day's activities to praise God for the gift of the day and ask him for the strength to continue serving him. These three times are morning, midday and evening. Many of us are used to praying at these times: the popular forms were morning prayers, the Angelus at noon, and prayers before we went to bed. Unfortunately, these venerable practices have fallen out of use to some extent. They provided a valuable service—they were "customary" prayer, which didn't require a lot of thought but served as reminders of the Lord's presence.

A more formal complement to these three prayer times developed early in the church's history. People came together at these times for communal prayer. This formal daily prayer made use of "the church's hymnal"—the book of psalms—and scripture. The hours were called morning prayer (lauds), daytime prayer (terce, sext, or none), and evening prayer (vespers). These prayer times, or "hours," were formalized into the divine office, and the book that contained them was called the breviary. Monasteries added other hours to these major times: vigils (matins, done very early in the morning), prime (after lauds, but before work began), and compline (or night prayer).

Everyone in sacred orders (deacons, priests and bishops) and many congregations of religious (monks, sisters, brothers) are bound to pray the office every day for the sake of, and in the name of, the church. But with the reform of the office and its renaming as the "Liturgy of the Hours," the church reminds us this responsibility is not a private duty of these groups. This prayer is a *liturgy*, and it should be done in community with members of the local church. The responsibility of those in holy orders has been widened. As the *General Instruction of the Liturgy of the Hours* (GILH) points out:

> Those in holy orders or with a special canonical mission have the responsibility of initiating and directing the prayer of the community. . . . They must therefore see to it that the faithful are invited—and prepared by suitable instruction—to celebrate the principal hours in common, especially on Sundays and feast days . . . so that they may be led by degrees to a greater appreciation and more frequent use of the prayer of the church (no. 23).

The reform of the Liturgy of the Hours indicates there are two principal hours: morning prayer and evening prayer. There are also three other (and minor) hours: office of readings, daytime prayer, and night prayer. Presently, two editions of the Liturgy of the Hours are available: the complete (four-volume) edition contains all the hours, and a one-volume edition contains morning prayer, evening prayer and some other elements of this official daily prayer of the church.

Praying the hours

More and more frequently, parishes and groups are finding the various hours a good way of praying in common—before or after meetings or adult education sessions, for instance. In some parishes, evening prayer on the Sundays of Lent has become an established custom. In other parishes, people are being introduced to the structure of the hours through the use of psalms and scripture reading combined with hymns and spontaneous prayer.

The *General Instruction of the Liturgy of the Hours* makes some points about the use of the psalms and other elements helpful in introducing the hours into a parish.

The psalms are a different kind of prayer from what we may be used to. For instance, they are not all addressed to God. Some are in dialogue form, some recount an event, etc. The psalms are sacred poetry, which "do not necessarily address God but are sung in God's presence" (GILH, no. 105). It is as if a good friend were with us. Sometimes we address the friend directly, sometimes we tell a story to our friend, sometimes we simply rejoice in the friend's presence. When we use the psalms this way, we represent the whole church. If a psalm's spirit does not accord with our emotions (e.g., it speaks of suffering when we are happy or at peace), we should remember we are expressing the "prayers and desires of all the Christian faithful" (GILH, no. 17). To help us understand the psalms in a Christian and messianic context, the hours provide a title for each, a prayer at the end, and an antiphon, to focus on the meaning (cf. GILH, nos. 110-120).

Besides the psalms, there are other hymns in the scriptures, and the Liturgy of the Hours makes use of these at morning prayer and evening prayer. In morning prayer, there is an Old Testament canticle inserted between the two psalms, and the Canticle of Zechariah (*Benedictus*) is prayed at the hour's conclusion. In evening prayer, a canticle from the epistles or the book of Revelation is placed after the two psalms, and the hour concludes with the Canticle of Mary (*Magnificat*). The gospel Canticle of Simeon (*Nunc dimittis*) is prayed at the end of night prayer.

Each hour begins with a hymn from the vast repertoire developed over the church's history. These hymns reflect the nature of the season, or the "feel" of the particular day or hour. As part of each hour, there is also a reading from scripture. These readings "unfold the mystery of Christ" during the liturgical year (GILH, no. 140). Although a brief reading is provided in the hour itself, a longer reading may be used when the hour is celebrated publicly (GILH, no. 142 and no. 46).

Morning prayer and evening prayer both conclude with a set of petitions. At morning prayer, these serve to dedicate the day to God, and at evening prayer they resemble the general intercessions at mass, praying for the needs of all men and women. These intercessions are followed by the Lord's Prayer, the common prayer of all the baptized, and the hours conclude with a "collect" or summary prayer.

Despite the protest that there is "no more time to be quiet in church," all the rites call for the use of silence during the church's worship. The Liturgy of the Hours calls silence necessary "to receive in our hearts the full resonance of the voice of the Holy Spirit and to unite our personal prayer more closely with the word of God and the public voice of the church" (GILH, no. 202).

Morning prayer and evening prayer

The *General Instruction* calls these two hours the "double hinge" of daily prayer (GILH, no. 37). They are the most important because they sum up the day's elements at its beginning and end. Morning prayer, for instance, dedicates the coming day to the Lord and recalls the Lord's resurrection (GILH, no. 38). Evening prayer is an opportunity to give thanks for the day and reminds us of the "evening sacrifice" of the Lord's supper. In the Eastern churches, it is tied to the symbol of light in the darkness, a powerful symbol of redemption at the Easter vigil (GILH, no. 39). These hours should be celebrated most frequently with the community.

The hours and the seasons

It will be some time before parishes institute the regular daily (or even weekly) celebration of the hours. But many parishes have had success in celebrating morning prayer and especially evening prayer during the great seasons of the church year. Some now pray evening prayer on the Sundays of Lent (and conclude the hour with benediction). This, it seems, would be a good way for a parish to introduce this prayer style. Gradually, the celebration of evening prayer could be widened to the Advent season, and then to days in the other great seasons—Epiphany during the Christmas season, or the feast of the Holy Family (when the blessing of families or of children could be part of the service), or Pentecost Sunday, at the conclusion of the Easter season.

Some effort must be made to invite people into this most ancient prayer form. Scriptural prayer, and regular, structured prayer, have been the mainstay of the church's life for generations, as well as the source for individual and private prayer. We cannot afford to lose these treasures.

Music, Art and Architecture

Here are three pictures. First, imagine 30,000 people gathered for the Super Bowl in January. Before the game begins, when excitement is at a fever pitch, the announcer says, "Please stand, and open your programs to page 12. We will now *recite* two verses of the *Star Spangled Banner*. Mahalia Jackson will lead us in this *recitation*."

Picture two. You are invited to a family's home for dinner. When you come in, there is no one to greet you, and no place to hang your coat. In the living room, there is only a hard wooden bench on which to sit, littered with the Sunday paper and used tissues.

The third picture. You go to visit an art gallery. All the artifacts are by third graders from the local school. Under each picture is a description which goes something like this: "*Morning Sunrise* by Chuckie Smith. In this painting, the artist is attempting to present his impression of what the sunrise looks like in the morning. The family cat is portrayed in the lower right corner. The artist's signature is in the lower left corner."

Silly, no? How long would people put up with this? Yet Sunday after Sunday, people who come to our churches live with these experiences.

Texts intended to be sung are recited, buildings seem designed to make people uncomfortable, and parishes seem determined to use artifacts no more interesting than a stop sign.

In earlier times, the church encouraged the arts and inspired artists to produce some of their best works—in music, drama, dance and the plastic arts (painting, statuary, mosaics, architecture). Once again, with the renewal of the basics of liturgy, the church has taken a stand in favor of the aesthetics of worship. The United States bishops have recognized that worship is itself an "art" which brings together the best human beings have to offer, so that liturgy's nature may shine beautifully and clearly. In the statement, *Environment and Art in Catholic Worship* (EAW), the bishops declare, "God does not need liturgy; people do, and people have only their own arts and styles of expression with which to celebrate" (no.4).

The seriousness with which we approach our worship, the beauty with which we endow it, and the richness of our symbols reflect the importance of what we do. If we are content with the second-best, the mediocre, the less-than-beautiful, we equate worship with the casual, mechanical parts of our life—with bus station waiting rooms and hamburgers gulped at fast-food stands, with road signs and telephone directories, with all that is non-essential, rushed, or taken for granted. If liturgy is what we claim, this is perhaps the worst disservice we can do it.

In recent years, the bishops, working with the national Federation of Diocesan Liturgical Commissions, have issued two statements on the importance of the arts and the way they serve our worship.

Music

The first statement was *Music in Catholic Worship* (MCW), issued in 1972. Music has "a preeminence among the arts of public worship" because it is the most "portable" of the arts—it can be employed anywhere there is a gathering of people to sing God's praises. Music has been integral to every human society and every form of worship. In Christian worship, however, clear principles need to be developed, so that it does indeed support what the community intends to do.

Those principles are described in *Music in Catholic Worship*. Music which serves worship must be quality music appropriate to the place at which it is used in liturgy and to the community that uses it. This means three judgments must be made about any piece of music: 1) The *musical judgment*—is it "technically, aesthetically, and expressively good" (whether folk or organ, choir or solo, congregational or instrumental) (MCW, no. 26)? 2) The *liturgical judgment*—does this music fit the general sense of the liturgy as well as its particular place in the liturgy (the "flow" of the rite, the sense of the text, the differentiation of roles in singing) (MCW nos. 31-38)? 3) The *pastoral judgment*—does it fit this celebration with this congregation (MCW no. 41)?

The statement also points out the need for a new model in planning music for worship, especially for the eucharist. In the past, we had two models: "high mass" with an ordinary and fourfold sung proper, and "low mass" with four hymns "that grew out of the Instruction on Sacred Music of 1958" (MCW, no. 52). This four-hymns model was developed for the Latin mass, and is now outdated. There are in the new order of mass more than a dozen places where music is appropriate, in addition to many options open to the celebrant. Aside from the celebrant's parts, these options fall into five categories, listed here in order of descending importance (the first set includes the *most* important places to sing; cf. MCW, nos. 50-74).

> *The acclamations.* These are "shouts of joy which arise from the whole assembly as forceful and meaningful assents to God's word and action" (MCW, no. 53). There are five in every eucharist: the gospel acclamation (alleluia), the three acclamations of the eucharistic prayer (seraphic hymn or "Holy, holy, holy," memorial acclamation, and great Amen), and the doxology to the Lord's Prayer. These should be sung "even at masses in which little else is sung" (MCW, no. 54).
>
> *Processional songs.* There are two places the order of mass calls for processional music: the entrance procession, and the communion procession. These two songs or chants "are very important for a sense of awareness of community" (MCW, no. 60).
>
> *Responsorial psalm.* Psalms were written to be sung, not recited. It makes no sense to respond to the first reading with another reading—the psalm. Whenever possible, the responsorial psalm should be sung (possibly with a seasonal refrain which the people could learn easily and repeat regularly).
>
> *Ordinary chants.* When there is singing, especially on festive occasions, it would be good to sing one or more of these com-

mon chants. However, only on rare occasions would they *all* be sung. These chants include: the "Lord, have mercy" (originally a "prayer of praise to the risen Christ"—MCW, no. 65), the "Glory to God," the "Lord's Prayer," the litany for the breaking of the bread ("Lamb of God"), and the profession of faith.

Supplementary songs. Listed here are places where there is no required text or even any indication there need be a spoken or sung text. But they are appropriate places for music or singing, especially by the choir: preparation of the altar and gifts (formerly known as the "offertory"), meditation time after communion, recessional, litanies (such as the general intercessions).

The principles in *Music in Catholic Worship* apply not only to eucharist, but to all the sacraments and the Liturgy of the Hours and paraliturgical services as well. To reduce these principles to basics, they are: sing what should be sung (what is important, what is written to be sung), sing it with respect to the diversity of ministries in the service, sing it *well* (good music, carefully done, adding to the beauty of the service).

Art and architecture

There are other arts almost as "portable" as music. Drama and ritual or rhythmic movement (dance) have been used most frequently in Catholic worship. Remnants of those arts are still visible in our worship—in processions, gestures, vestments, the dramatic services of the Easter Triduum. Like many other signs and art forms, these have been afflicted with a certain "minimalism" that has reduced them to a least common denominator. In that form we have received them from the ages before us. We are just now beginning to recover those arts that use the human body and the human voice to praise God.

Very early, human culture learned that the arts and worship seemed to work best in a space designed for them. This hard-learned lesson gave us the great buildings of human civilizations, especially the churches of Christendom. At first, these buildings were simply the skins for liturgical action—fairly bare spaces in which the liturgy itself provided the color and decoration, places for "praying and singing, for listening and speaking"—places "for human interaction and active participation" (EAW no. 39).

Gradually, the importance of the event led to a sense of the importance of the building and artifacts used in worship. The importance and beauty of the action soon dictated the space itself should be highlighted by painting, mosaic and sculpture. The altar had to reflect the "weight" of the eucharistic action, as did the reading desk (ambo or lectern) and the bishop's chair. The people decorated themselves with their best clothes. The bread and wine had to be the best and richest the community could offer, and even the gifts of earth (green plants, spring flowers, palms) were brought to enhance the place of worship.

As the rites were minimalized ("breadless" hosts, "silent" masses, the pouring of a few drops of water at baptism), the space for worship and the artifacts were maximalized. Beauty was transferred to the walls. Chalices were made of gold, decorated with jewels. Vestments were woven from cloth of gold. There was a certain amount of beauty inherent in what the Christian community was doing, and it had to come out somewhere. If it disappeared from one place, it was bound to spring up in another.

What does this mean for our worship? Several things, as indicated by the bishops in *Environment and Art in Catholic Worship* (published in 1978). The place we must first search for beauty is the liturgy itself. Music, gesture, proclamation, preaching, silence, posture—these are the beautiful actions of the "saints" (EAW nos. 27-38). The other arts serve this beauty.

The worship space, no matter how old or new, should be hospitable and open. There the assembly of the baptized gather to form the Body of Christ. It must have human qualities and a human scale, so the community's work may be seen and heard (EAW nos. 40-54).

The furnishings and objects used by this community must have a dignity and beauty appropriate to the event, and must clearly reflect the meaning of the rites in which they are used. A font in which no one can be immersed is inappropriate. A chalice from which only one person can drink is inappropriate. Benches or chairs which make people uncomfortable are inappropriate (EAW nos. 63-106).

The final paragraph of *Environment and Art* (no. 107) is a perfect summary:

> When the Christian community gathers to celebrate its faith and vision, it gathers to celebrate what is most personally theirs and most nobly human and truly church. The actions of the

assembly witness the great deeds God has done; they confirm an age-old covenant. With such vision and depth of the assembly can the environment be anything less than a vehicle to meet the Lord and to encounter one another?

Devotions

Devotions, like the rosary and novenas, developed out of people's need for prayer forms other than those provided in the liturgy. The official liturgy cannot (and should not) try to encompass all prayer needs. There should be room through popular devotions for people to develop their special interests and styles of prayer. However, because some devotions do reflect elements of the liturgy, they should be in line with the liturgical year and the liturgical rites. Thus, the development of the "scriptural rosary" and Lenten devotions, as well as semi-official rites such as the Advent wreath, reflect the concerns of the liturgy. One area that requires special attention is devotion to the reserved eucharist outside mass. Because this relates directly to the eucharist's place in people's lives, a special part of the revised ritual is devoted to this devotion.

Exposition (Forty Hours)

The practice of lengthy exposition of the blessed sacrament is encouraged "only if suitable numbers of the faithful are expected to be present" (*General Introduction to Holy Communion and Worship of the Eucharist*

Outside of Mass—GIHC—no. 86). If the sacrament cannot be exposed for the full length of this particular devotion, because of small numbers in attendance or other intervening services, then it may be replaced in the tabernacle, using the simple form of reposition (GIHC, no. 88). The reserved sacrament is *not* to be exposed while mass is celebrated in the body of the church (GIHC, no. 83).

Brief period of exposition (benediction)

What is said here applies to all forms of exposition, either lengthy or short, but most people will probably experience the change in benedictions most clearly. There are some physical changes in the practice. Exposition held "exclusively for the giving of benediction is prohibited" (GIHC, no. 89). "A single genuflection is made in the presence of the blessed sacrament, whether reserved in the tabernacle or exposed for public adoration" (GIHC, no. 84). The sacrament may be exposed in a monstrance (four to six candles are lighted, incense is used, the priest or deacon wears alb or cassock and surplice, stole, cope and humeral veil) or in the ciborium (at least two candles are lighted, incense may be used, the minister wears the appropriate liturgical vestments, and the priest or deacon wears the humeral veil for the benediction). Cf. GIHC, nos. 85, 91 and 92.

The new rite for exposition and benediction has four parts:

> *exposition* (preparatory rites, which might include an opening song, the bringing of the sacrament from the tabernacle to the altar, placing the host in the monstrance, and incensation);

> *adoration* (which should include "prayers, songs, and readings to direct the attention of the faithful to the worship of Christ the Lord," GIHC, no. 95, and which may include a homily and time spent in "religious silence"—this may take the form of one of the hours, especially the principal ones, morning or evening prayer);

> *benediction* (which includes a eucharistic song, incensation, a prayer from the options offered in GIHC no. 98, and the silent blessing with the sacrament);

> *reposition* (which concludes the service).

Obviously, the outline's second part—adoration—has been expanded in

Bibliography

A parish should have resources on hand for its liturgy team. This selected list describes some basic materials that offer background information and planning helps.

For historical study, the best work on the Roman rite remains Joseph Jungmann's *Mass of the Roman Rite*, first published in English in two volumes (1951). That two-volume edition is now rare, but the one-volume abridgement is still available. Jungmann's *The Mass* (1976, Liturgical Press) is also helpful.

Texts

General Instruction of the Roman Missal (1973, U.S.C.C. Publications Office, 1312 Massachusetts Avenue, N.W., Washington, D.C. 20005). This document, basic to the eucharistic liturgy, is also printed in the front of the *Sacramentary*.

Directory for Masses with Children (U.S.C.C. Publications). This text too is in the front of the *Sacramentary*.

The Rites (1976, Pueblo Publishing Company, 1860 Broadway, New
York, N.Y. 10023). This study edition of all the rites contains
their introductions and prayers but not the texts of the scripture
readings. It does not include the order of mass or the liturgy of
the hours.

The Liturgy of the Hours. The approved complete edition is available in
four volumes from the Catholic Book Publishing Company.
Several editions in one volume give the complete texts for
morning prayer and evening prayer.

Commentaries

The New Order of Mass, edited by J. Patino (1970, The Liturgical Press,
Collegeville, MN. 56321). This edition contains the official
Latin text, an unofficial English translation, and a helpful
commentary on the *General Instruction of the Roman Missal.*

Music in Catholic Worship (1972, U.S.C.C. Publications). A statement
from the Bishops' Committee on the Liturgy.

Environment and Art in Catholic Worship (1978, U.S.C.C. Publications).
A statement from the Bishops' Committee on the Liturgy.

Rite of Anointing and Pastoral Care of the Sick: Background Catechesis
(1973, Federation of Diocesan Liturgical Commissions, 1307
South Wabash, Chicago, IL. 60605).

Rite of Penance: Background Catechesis (1974, Federation of Diocesan Liturgical Commissions).

Study Texts (U.S.C.C. Publications). The Bishops' Committee on the
Liturgy publishes a continuing series of background studies on
the various rites and liturgical questions.

Other

Catholic Liturgy Book, Ralph Keifer, general editor (1975, Helicon Press,
Baltimore). Designed as a service book and hymnal, it contains
useful commentaries on the rites and the liturgical year.

Celebrating the Saints (1978, Pueblo Publishing Company). A collection
of texts and bibliographies for saints' feasts.

Crotty, R. and Manly, G., *Commentaries on the Readings of the Lectionary* (1978, Pueblo Publishing Company).

Deiss, Lucien, *Biblical Prayers* (1976, World Library Publications, 2145 Central Parkway, Cincinnati, OH. 45214). This collection of scripturally based prayers and intercessions is a good resource for weekday liturgy.

————— , *Spirit and Song of the New Liturgy* (1970 World Library Publications).

Faucher, T. and Neiland, I.C., *Touching God* (1975, Ave Maria Press, Notre Dame, IN. 46556). This children's liturgy book has excellent introductory material. Its principles will help you evaluate the many other books of "sample" children's liturgies now on the market.

Freburger, W., *This Is the Word of the Lord* (1974, Ave Maria Press). Selected scripture texts from the three-year cycle arranged for three-part reading.

————— , and Haas, J., *Eucharistic Prayers for Children* (1976, Ave Maria Press). Contains commentaries of the three eucharistic prayers and thematic liturgies derived from the prayers.

Gelineau, J., *The Liturgy Today and Tomorrow* (1978, Paulist Press, 545 Island Road, Ramsey, N.J. 07446).

Hartgen, W., *Planning Guide for Lent and Holy Week* (1979, Pastoral Arts Associates, 4744 West Country Gables Drive, Glendale, AZ. 85306).

Hovda, R., Strong, *Loving and Wise: Presiding in Liturgy* (The Liturgical Conference, 810 Rhode Island Avenue, N.E., Washington, D.C. 20018).

Mitchell, L., *The Meaning of Ritual* (1977, Paulist Press).

Parish Liturgy Committee Handbook (1975, The Liturgical Conference). A nine-week study course for committee members.

Prayers of the Faithful (1977, Pueblo Publishing Company). A good collection to work *from* in preparing the general intercessions.

This Far by Faith (The Liturgical Conference). A good introduction to the worship style of black communities and the reasons for it.

Touchstones for Liturgical Ministries (1978, The Liturgical Conference). Single sheet tear-out pages for the various liturgical ministries.

Tucciarone, A. and Cafardi, N., *Copyright and the Church Musician* (1977, Diocese of Pittsburgh, 111 Boulevard of Allies, Pittsburgh, PA. 15222). Most complete explanation available about the copyright laws.

Walsh, E., *A Theology of Celebration* (Pastoral Arts Associates).

————, *The Ministry of the Celebrating Community* (Pastoral Arts Associates).

————, *Practical Suggestions for Celebrating Sunday Mass* (Pastoral Arts Associates).

————, *The Order of Mass: Guidelines* (Pastoral Arts Associates).